For You,
My Daughter

For You, My Daughter

A collection of poems
Edited by Susan Polis Schutz

Blue Mountain Press ™

Boulder, Colorado

Library of Congress Number: 84-71906
ISBN: 0-88396-222-5

The following works have previously appeared in Blue Mountain Arts publications:

"I will support you," by Susan Polis Schutz. Copyright © Continental Publications, 1979. "I am always here," by Susan Polis Schutz. Copyright © Stephen Schutz and Susan Polis Schutz, 1982. "More Than You Know . . .," by Andrew Tawney. Copyright © Blue Mountain Arts, Inc., 1982. "To My Daughter," by Susan Polis Schutz. Copyright © Stephen Schutz and Susan Polis Schutz, 1983. "Don't Ever . . .," by Laine Parsons. Copyright © Blue Mountain Arts, Inc., 1983. "Dear Daughter," by Anna Edwards; "My dear daughter . . .," by Carol Ann Bader; "Daughter, I Want You to Know . . .," by M. Joye; "Whenever life is getting you down," by Lindsay Newman; "Daughter, You Are Loved," by Roger Pinches; "I hope that today," by Susie Schneider; "Child of Mine," by Laine Parsons; and "Daughter," by Rosemary DePaolis. Copyright © Blue Mountain Arts, Inc., 1984. All rights reserved.

Thanks to the Blue Mountain Arts creative staff.

ACKNOWLEDGMENTS appear on page 62.

Manufactured in the United States of America
Thirteenth Printing: February 1999

 This book is printed on recycled paper.

Blue Mountain Press INC.

P.O. Box 4549, Boulder, Colorado 80306

CONTENTS

My dear daughter . . .

I want so much for you to know
how much I love you.

I am critical of you sometimes, but
it's only because I have experienced
so much more of life, and I can often
see that the path you are taking
today, may not take you to where
you want to be tomorrow.

I know, too, that you are still young,
and you have to experience life for
yourself. If I can . . .

I just want to spare you some of
the pain I had to go through on my
own path in life . . .

When the words don't come with all I
want to say, I can still say this:
I love you tremendously. I would do
anything for you. And I promise I will
try to be more patient and understanding
of you, and I pray that you will do the
same for me.

And do me a favor sometimes . . .
tell me you love me, okay?
Having you grow up so quickly
is hard on me.

— Carol Ann Bader

Daughter, I Want You to Know . . .

It's hard sometimes, when people
are changing their lives, to
understand each other, or even
to talk. You are struggling right
now for independence and the
right to live your own way . . .
and I sometimes struggle for
the strength to let you do it.
I wish now and then for the days
when a kiss or a hug could make
your world bright again; but
your world is more difficult now,
and you want to make your own
way in it — which is as it should be.
I only want you to know . . .
that when you get hurt, I will
hurt for you; and that deep
down, I always have confidence
in your ability to find your place
in your world. If you ever need a
caring heart, or someone to listen
to your deepest dreams or concerns,
I will be there for you;
and remember, above all else . . .
that I love and care for you.

— M. Joye

To My Daughter

When you were born
I held you in my arms
and just kept smiling at you
You always smiled back
your big eyes wide open
full of love
You were such a
beautiful
good
sweet baby
Now
as I
watch you
grow up
and become your
own person. . .

I look at you
your laughter
your happiness
your simplicity
your beauty
and I wonder
where you will be
in fifteen years
and I wonder
where the world will be
in fifteen years
I just hope
that you will
be able to
enjoy a life
of sensitivity
goodness
accomplishment
and love
in a world
that is at peace
But most of all
I want you to know that
I am very proud
of you
and that I
love you dearly

— Susan Polis Schutz

Whenever life is getting you down, daughter,
   remember this . . .

To solve each problem one at a time;
to take each day as it comes.
To stick to your goals, no matter
   what happens,
and press on toward your dreams.
To keep your attention focused on
   the future,
as you consider the solutions at hand.
To look for the bright side,
even though it may be temporarily
   covered by a cloud.
To smile often, even when a frown
   feels more natural.
To think of those you love,
   and know that they love you, too.

No matter how difficult it may seem,
you have within you the power,
   the ability,
      and the knowledge
to make things better.

— Lindsay Newman

I hope that today
    and always
the love I have for you
is reaching out
and touching you —
        making your days
            a little brighter
        and your heart
            a little warmer.

I hope that today
    and always
you are aware of how
special you are to me,
and how lucky I feel
        to have you in my life.

— Susie Schneider

Don't Ever . . .

Don't ever try to understand everything —
    some things will just never make sense.
Don't ever be reluctant to show your feelings —
    when you're happy, give into it!
    When you're not, live with it.
Don't ever be afraid to try to make things better —
    you might be surprised at the results.
Don't ever take the weight of the world
    on your shoulders.
Don't ever feel threatened by the future —
    take life one day at a time.   *God is in control*
Don't ever feel guilty about the past —   *of tomorrow.*
    what's done is done. Learn from any mistakes
    you might have made.
Don't ever feel that you are alone —
    there is always somebody there for you
    to reach out to.
Don't ever forget that you can achieve
    so many of the things you can imagine —
    imagine that! It's not as hard as it seems.
Don't ever stop loving,
    don't ever stop believing,
        don't ever stop dreaming your dreams.

— Laine Parsons

Daughter, You Are Loved

When the road seems too long
When darkness sets in
When everything turns out wrong
And you can't find a friend
Remember — you are loved

When smiles are hard to come by
And you're feeling down
When you spread your wings to fly
And can't get off the ground
Remember — you are loved

When time runs out before you're through
And it's over before you begin
When little things get to you
And you just can't win
Remember — you are loved . . .

When your loved ones are far away
And you are on your own
When you don't know what to say
When you're afraid of being alone
Remember — you are loved

When your sadness comes to an end
And everything is going right
May you think of your family and friends
And keep their love in sight
A thank-you for being loved

May you see the love around you
In everything you do
And when troubles seem to surround you
May all the love shine through
You are blessed — you are loved

— Roger Pinches

I wish you the courage to be warm
when the world would prefer that you
    be cool.
I wish you success sufficient to your
    needs; I wish you failure to
    temper that success.
I wish you joy in all your days; I
    wish you sadness so that you
    may better measure joy.
I wish you gladness to overbalance
    grief.
I wish you humor and a twinkle in
    the eye.
I wish you glory and the strength to
    bear its burdens.
I wish you sunshine on your path
    and storms to season your
    journey . . .

I wish you peace — in the world in
   which you live and in the
   smallest corner of the heart
   where truth is kept.
I wish you faith — to help define
   your living and your life.
· More I cannot wish you — except
   perhaps love — to make all
   the rest worthwhile.

— Robert A. Ward

Seek wisdom to know who you are!

19

I am always here
to understand you
I am always here
to laugh with you
I am always here
to cry with you
I am always here
to talk to you
I am always here
to think with you
I am always here
to plan with you
Even though we
might not always
be together
please know that
I am always
here to
love
you

— Susan Polis Schutz

You have powers you never dreamed of. You can do things you never thought you could do. There are no limitations in what you can do except the limitations in your own mind as to what you cannot do.
　　Don't think you cannot.
　　Think you can.

— Darwin P. Kingsley

This is the beginning of a new, broader, yet focused path — bloom little bud!

I will support you
in all that you
do
I will help you
in all that you
need
I will share with you
in all that you
experience
I will encourage you
in all that you
try
I will understand you
in all that is in your
heart
I will love you
in all that you
are

— Susan Polis Schutz

i wish for you warmth
when it is cold outside

i wish for you a star
when the night is dark

i wish for you courage
when the world is afraid

i think of you, i wish for you
and i hope you know —
that here, there is a heart
and a home;
and here, there is someone
who loves you
more than any wish could
ever give.

— laura west

Even
if a day
should go by
when I don't say
"I love you . . ."

May never a
moment go by
without you
knowing I do

— Daniel Haughian

Daughter,
You Are Special

"Special" is a word
that is used to describe
something one-of-a-kind
like a hug
or a sunset
or a person who spreads love
with a smile or kind gesture.
"Special" describes people
who act from the heart
and keep in mind the hearts
    of others.
"Special" applies to something
that is admired and precious
and which can never be replaced.
"Special" is the word that best
    describes you.

— Teri Fernandez

Remember . . .

If ever you need to talk,
 to share a laugh,
 a dream, a smile;
to be comforted
or reassured,
to be understood . . .

Remember,
my shoulder is there
 for your head,
your secrets are safe
and my door
is always open.

— Ronda Scott

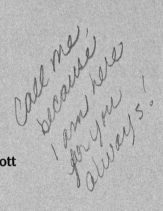

When you are hurting
   it is so hard to know
   that you are struggling . . .
I want to lift you up
   to a place of sunshine
   and mountaintops.
I know that sometimes
   the greatest gift I can give you
   is to leave you alone,
But when you need somebody,
         remember that
            I'll be there
            to lift you up.

— Sue Mitchell

Gentle Words of Encouragement

Spend every day preparing for the next.

As you reach forward with one hand, accept
the advice of those who have gone
before you, and in the same manner
reach back with the other hand to those
who follow you; for life is a fragile chain
of experiences held together by love.
Take pride in being a strong link in that
chain. Discipline yourself, but do not be
harsh. The pleasures of life are yours to
be taken. Share them with others, but
always remember that you, too, have
earned the right to partake.

Know those who love you; love is the finest
of all gifts and is received only to be
given. Embrace those who truly love
you; for they are few in a lifetime . . .

Jen,
you
are a
give, so →

Then return that love tenfold, radiating it
from your heart to fill their lives as sunlight
warms the darkest corners of the earth.
Love is a journey, not a destination;
travel its path daily. Do this and your
troubles will be as fleeting as footprints
in the sand. When loneliness is your
companion and all about you seem to be
gone, pause and listen, for the sound of
loneliness is silence, and in silence we
hear best. Listen well, and your
moments of silence will always be
broken by the gentle words of
encouragement spoken by those of us
who love you.

Listen to God say "I love you"

— Tim Murtaugh

My Family

There is an
irreplaceable feeling
that I wouldn't give up for the world —
a sense of belonging,
of being able to turn
to the outstretched hands
   of those I love . . . at any time;
to know they'll understand me,
   and comfort me
   when things go wrong,
or laugh with me
   when things make me happy.
Caring and sharing
   life's ups and downs,
and mostly,
   loving . . .
as I so dearly love them.

— Debbie Avery

I ask myself
why I have been
    blessed with someone
    so understanding
    and so caring . . .
Perhaps it's because
I can truly appreciate you
or maybe it's because
    God knew
    I needed you
    so much.

— Jean Therese

Dear Daughter,

I worry sometimes that I pushed
   too hard
when you were growing up —
wanting so much for you
and trying to make sure you had
all those things that I didn't
   when I was a child.
But I hope that I never made you
feel that I expected too much . . .
for no matter what you become
   or what you achieve,
what matters most to me is that
   you're happy
and that I'm never without your
   love.

I'll always be here for you . . .
   no matter what you do.

— Anna Edwards

Child of Mine

It's been so gratifying
for me to see you
go through such positive changes
    and inner growth.
Your happiness is contagious,
    and I'm so happy for you . . .
to see you becoming
        a strong individual
and doing all the right things
to make your days ahead
    shine even brighter.

It's been great for me
to watch you grow
and to become
even more of that special someone
        you are . . . inside . . .

Through your growing and changing,
I want to ask that you
    take me along with you.
I don't mean that I want you
to tell me every thought
    you have along the way,
but to remember that I am here . . .
    wherever and whenever you need me.
And I hope that you'll remember
    that I'm on your side.
And even if I can't always help you win,
there will never be a day
        when I won't be
                    cheering you on.

— Laine Parsons

Daughter, You're a Winner . . .

A winner sweats
when no one is looking,
finds strength and courage
when all seems lost.

Pain is never on her mind,
but always in her body.

Her strongest muscle, her heart,
knows no rest, for it is
continually striving towards
its goal.

A winner has pride in her soul
and humility in her step.

A winner always comes back,
even when the score says
differently,
just to prove that she's a winner.

And you will always be a winner.

— Sara L. Brandon

My Darling Daughter

You are a shining
example of what a
daughter can be —
love and laughter
beautiful and good
honest and principled
determined and independent
sensitive and intelligent
You are a shining
example of what every
mother wishes her
daughter was
and I
am so very
proud of
you

— Susan Polis Schutz

To My Daughter, with Love

May the wind carry you
  to safe and distant shores
and the moon and stars be your
  faithful guides.
May the child in you never stop
  questioning,
your soul always be peaceful
  and free.
May you find the strength within you
  when life calls for it
and have the ability to control
  your weaknesses.
May your heart be filled with love
  and with pride,
as mine is today
  when I think of you, my daughter.

— Mary Ann Pantano

While you are
finding yourself in the world,
there are many rewards in life.
Happiness awaits you,
and there are joys
    to give and to receive.
There is knowledge to be found.
Always listen to your own heart
    while reaching for
        nothing but the best.
Give to life,
and life will give to you.
And as you live, always remember
    that you are loved.

— Gwenda Jennings

In this special moment in life . . .

Think freely. Practice patience.
Smile often. Savor special moments.
Live God's message. Make new
friends. Rediscover old ones. Tell
those you love that you do. Feel
deeply. Forget trouble. Forgive an
enemy. Hope. Grow. Be crazy. Count
your blessings. Observe miracles.
Make them happen. Discard worry.
Give. Give in. Trust enough to take.
Pick some flowers. Share them. Keep
a promise. Look for rainbows. Gaze
at stars. See beauty everywhere.
Work hard. Be wise. Try to
understand. Take time for people.
Make time for yourself. Laugh
heartily. Spread joy. Take a chance.
Reach out. Let someone in. Try
something new. Slow down. Be soft
sometimes. Believe in yourself. Trust
others. See a sunrise. Listen to rain.
Reminisce. Cry when you need to.
Trust life. Have faith. Enjoy wonder.
Comfort a friend. Have good ideas.
Make some mistakes. Learn from
them. Celebrate life.

— Jan Michelsen

There are so many things
I can't do . . . so many things I'll never be . . .
but I can write a poem and sew a shirt.
I can cook your favorite meal
and find pleasure in walking with you
along a country road, sharing the
beauty that means so much to us.
I can encourage you when you're down
and be happy for you when you're up . . .
and I can love you
every minute
of my life.

— Virginia Richardson

Remember this, my daughter . . .

There is no difficulty that enough love
will not conquer; No disease that enough
love will not heal; No door that enough love
will not open; No gulf that enough love will
not bridge; No wall that enough love will not
throw down; No sin that enough love
will not redeem . . .

It makes no difference how deeply
seated may be the trouble;
How hopeless the outlook; How muddled
the tangle; How great the mistake.
A sufficient realization of love will dissolve
it all . . . If only you could love enough you
would be the happiest and most powerful
being in the world . . .

— Emmet Fox

On Being a Parent

You must know, my child,
that much of the strength
    of my life
is in the love I have for you.
I look in the mirror,
and what do I see . . .
    just an ordinary parent
trying to do the best she can.
But more than words can say,
    I need you in my life.
For all the things I've tried
    to give to you, you have
given me . . .
    courage
        and feeling
            and determination.

So this is for you
    with great love
        and hugs and kisses . . .
            from your mom.

— Sabrina O'Neal

To Daughter,

I remember so well our first meeting.
I looked into your trusting eyes,
and you captured my heart.
Your tiny hands reached out
and gave me warmth and purpose.
The years since have passed so quickly —
filled with happiness and love.
No mother could ask for more in a
   daughter.
I recall again that first meeting,
with love and pride to be your mom.

— Margaret Benson

My darling daughter
I am so glad that
you were born today
when women are so
aware of what is going on
and don't always have
to fight so hard to be heard
The world is wide open
for you to be whatever you want
It will be hard
but at least you
will find other women
striving for the same things
 and you won't be called "crazy"
for wanting to achieve them
Though full equality
is a long way off
there certainly have been changes
which would make your life as a woman
not so stereotyped and confined
My darling daughter
you are living in an age
where womanhood is finally growing
to be everything
that it can be

— Susan Polis Schutz

I Know . . .

Sometimes the world
     seems so cold.
There are moments when
   you try your best,
and even that isn't good enough.
You yearn for the best
   life has to offer,
but you wonder if it will ever appear.

But *you have to keep believing* . . .
   you have to remember
that things *will* get better,
   that you will find strength,
     and you have to
        believe in yourself . . .

   the way that I
     believe in you.

          — Gina Bowie

What I want for you
is your freedom.
Most of the time I know
you must stand alone.
But if there's room for
a foot by you
and you need it,
I want my foot there.
And when you need
to be by yourself,
I want you to be
by yourself.

— Mary Haskell

More Than You Know . . . Daughter

I'd like to tell you
how much I love you,
and I hope you know that I do . . .
I wish that the words I speak
   so gently to you could be
heard by your heart
   with the same meanings
and the same soft feelings of love
that they carry from deep within me.

For more than you know . . .
   I love so many things about you.
   I enjoy sharing life with you.
I enjoy the way we balance each other out,
how we share the good times
   and support each other through the tears. . .

I enjoy the knowledge that we'll make it
    through whatever life brings
with courage and with love
through the years.

More than you know . . .
    and more than I can ever say,
I feel a wonderful thankfulness
    in my heart . . . just for you.
And I want you to remember, though
    my thoughts don't always convey
    and my feelings don't always show,
I love you, and I always will . . .
    more than you know.

— Andrew Tawney

When the world closes in
and lies so heavily upon you . . .
remember that I care.
When the ones with whom you
share your life seem like strangers . . .
remember that I care.
When love seems to only bring
you pain . . .
remember that I care.
What cannot be, cannot be.
But always remember, I care.
Never be afraid to come to me,
if you have need of the
   simplest thing.
No matter what it is . . .
     I care.

— Kathy Boss

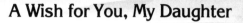

A Wish for You, My Daughter

If there could be only one thing
   in life for me to teach you,
I would teach you to love . . .

To respect others so that you may
   find respect in yourself
To learn the value of giving,
    so that if ever there comes a time
    in your life that someone really
    needs, you will give
To act in a manner that you would
   wish to be treated; to be proud
   of yourself
To laugh and smile as much as you
   can, in order to help bring joy
   back into this world
To have faith in others;
   to be understanding
To stand tall in this world and
   to learn to depend on yourself. . .

To only take from this earth
those things which you really
need, so there will be enough
for others
To not depend on money or
material things for your
happiness, but
To learn to appreciate the people
who love you, the simple beauty
that God gave you and to find
peace and security within
yourself

To you, my child, I hope I have
taught all of these things,
for they are love.

— Donna Dargis

To My Daughter

Since you were born
you have been
such a beautiful
addition to our family
Now that you are growing up
I can see that
you are a beautiful
addition to the world
and I am so
proud of you
As we watch you
doing things on your own . . .

we know you will find
happiness and success
because we are confident in
your ability
your self-knowledge
your values
But if you ever need a boost
or just someone to talk to
about difficulties that might be occurring
we are always here
to help you
to understand you
to support you
and to love
you

— Susan Polis Schutz

Daughter

Goals are dreams and wishes
    that are not easily reached.
You have to work hard to
        obtain them,
    never knowing when
        or where
    you will reach your goal.

    But keep trying!
    Do not give up hope.
    And most of all . . .

never stop
      believing in yourself.

For within you
there is someone
      special . . .

someone wonderful
      and successful.
No matter what you achieve,
   as long as you want it
      and it makes you
         happy,

you are a success.

— Rosemary DePaolis

ACKNOWLEDGMENTS

We gratefully acknowledge the permission granted by the following authors, publishers and authors' representatives to reprint poems and excerpts from their publications.

Robert A. Ward for "I wish you the courage." Copyright © Robert A. Ward, 1980. All rights reserved. Reprinted by permission.

Laura West for "i wish for you warmth." Copyright © Laura West, 1982. All rights reserved. Reprinted by permission.

Daniel Haughian for "Even if a day." Copyright © Daniel Haughian, 1981. All rights reserved. Reprinted by permission.

Teri Fernandez for "Daughter, You Are Special." Copyright © Teri Fernandez, 1983. All rights reserved. Reprinted by permission.

Ronda Scott for "Remember . . . If ever you need to talk." Copyright © Ronda Scott, 1982. All rights reserved. Reprinted by permission.

Sue Mitchell for "When you are hurting." Copyright © Sue Mitchell, 1981. All rights reserved. Reprinted by permission.

Tim Murtaugh for "Gentle Words of Encouragement." Copyright © Tim Murtaugh, 1983. All rights reserved. Reprinted by permission.

Debbie Avery for "My Family." Copyright © Debbie Avery, 1984. All rights reserved. Reprinted by permission.

Jean Therese for "I ask myself." Copyright © Jean Therese, 1981. All rights reserved. Reprinted by permission.

Sara L. Brandon for "Daughter, You're a Winner." Copyright © Sara L. Brandon, 1984. All rights reserved. Reprinted by permission.

Mary Ann Pantano for "To My Daughter, with Love." Copyright © Mary Ann Pantano, 1984. All rights reserved. Reprinted by permission.

This book is printed on fine quality, laid embossed, 80 lb. paper. This paper has been specially produced to be acid free (neutral pH) and contains no groundwood or unbleached pulp. It conforms with all of the requirements of the American National Standards Institute, Inc., so as to ensure that this book will last and be enjoyed by future generations.